Ms. Cordova

S C I E N C E
Mini-Mysteries

SCIENCE
Mini-Mysteries

by Sandra Markle

Atheneum   1988   New York

For my son, Scott,
whose room is always full of mysteries,
particularly under the bed.

Atheneum
Macmillan Publishing Company
866 Third Avenue, New York, NY 10022
Collier Macmillan Canada, Inc.
Type set by Arcata Graphics/Kingsport, Kingsport, Tennessee
Printed and bound by Book Press, Brattleboro, Vermont
Designed by Mary Ahern
First Edition
10 9 8 7 6 5 4 3 2 1

Library of Congress Cataloging-in-Publication Data
Markle, Sandra   Science mini-mysteries.
Includes index
SUMMARY: Provides instructions for twenty-nine scientific experiments,
tricks, and effects, in which the reader is challenged to explain or predict the
final outcome.
1. Science—Experiments—Juvenile literature.   2. Scientific recreations—
Juvenile literature. [1. Science—Experiments.   2. Scientific recreations.
3. Experiments] I. Title.
Q164.M275   1988   507.8   87-17420
ISBN 0-689-31291-1

Contents

Getting Started

Do you like working puzzles? Do brain teasers get you thinking? Do you enjoy trying to figure out who did it as you watch detective shows? Then these science mysteries are for you.

These aren't your usual hands-on activities. Each one is an investigation with a twist. Sometimes an experiment is in progress, and you have to figure out what will happen next. Other times, you're shown a completed activity. Then your job is to discover what happened to cause those results. You may be given a set of materials that can be used to produce something. But you have to figure out how to put these items together. You'll search for ways to change some experiments and try to discover missing parts of others. You'll even be shown investigations that didn't work as expected, and you'll be challenged to find out what went wrong.

This book is packed with science action designed to keep you guessing. The solutions are always just one page away, but no fair peeking. Collect the clues and investigate. Here's your chance to be a science detective. So see how many of the mini-mysteries you can solve.

Good luck!

Using Good Scientific Method

Here's a list every science detective should keep handy. When you work on an experiment, check to be sure you've covered each of these points. Then you can be sure all your clues are reliable.

1 *Control all the variables other than the one being tested. Think about everything that could change in your experiment. Anything that can change is called a variable. Then be sure that all the variables except the one being investigated are kept exactly the same throughout the tests.*

2 *Change the variable being investigated in a logical, orderly way. For example, you could test an electromagnet's strength with five, ten, and fifteen coils. This would let you see if having more coils made the electromagnet stronger.*

3 *Be sure there is a control. The control is the part of the experiment that has all of the variables regulated so the conditions are most nearly normal. Having a control lets you compare what happens in your test to what could usually be expected to happen.*

4 *Repeat the control and the tests. This should be done at least three times. The more times you repeat and obtain the same results, the surer you can be that you've observed what will usually happen. Something that happens only once could just be a freak occurrence.*

5 *Be a good observer. Make all measurements as exact as possible.*

1.
The String Trick

This ice cube is hanging by a thread. Do you think the glue, the salt, the sugar, or the tape was used to stick the thread to the ice?

You'll need four ice cubes and four pieces of thread, each about 10 inches long, to find the sticky solution to this mystery. Keep each ice cube cold until you are ready to experiment. Place the test cube on a piece of waxed paper. Wet the end of one piece of thread by dipping it into a glass of water.

Next, coil about 2 inches of the wet thread on top of the cube, and put the test material on top of the thread. For the salt and sugar, sprinkle on about ¼ teaspoonful each. Count to ten to allow the glue to set or the other materials to react with the ice. Then pull the free end of the thread up slowly. If the thread doesn't stick, test the next cube with another material and another piece of thread. Check the solution below to find out which material does the trick and why it works.

SOLUTION:

The salt makes the thread stick to the ice cube. This happens because salt lowers the freezing temperature of water. In other words, fresh water freezes at 32° F., but saltwater has to be colder than that to freeze. So where the salt touches the cube, the ice melts. The water that is produced usually runs off, carrying most of the salt away. Then the cube itself is cold enough to refreeze the remaining water. This glaze of ice anchors the thread to the cube.

2.
The Case of the Bubbling Glass

Both of the glasses pictured below contain yeast and water. Only one contains sugar. Do you think the foaming glass is the one with or without sugar?

THE CASE OF THE BUBBLING GLASS SOLUTION

Try the experiment to find out if you're right. After you've discovered what happens, check the explanation at the bottom of the page. You'll need two packages of yeast, a bowl, a measuring cup, water, two glasses, 1 tablespoon of sugar, and a spoon. Then follow the steps below.

1 *Pour the yeast into the bowl. Add 1 cup of warm water and stir to dissolve the yeast. Pour half of this solution into each of the glasses.*

2 *Add 1 tablespoon of sugar to one of the glasses and stir. Then let both glasses sit in a warm spot. Check every ten minutes.*

SOLUTION:

Yeast is a plant. Like all plants, yeast needs to be warm and have plenty of water to grow. Unlike a green plant, a yeast plant can't make its own food. The sugar supplies the food the yeast needs to grow. As it grows, the yeast plant changes the sugar into carbon dioxide gas and alcohol. So the foamy glass is the one that contains sugar. The foam is really bubbles of gas. Yeast is used to make bread because the bubbles given off by the growing yeast plants make the dough rise. You have probably seen holes in bread. These formed when gas bubbles popped. When bread is baked, the heat drives off the alcohol and kills the yeast plants.

3.
Magic Air

This experiment is a test to find out what happens to air when it becomes warm. The neck of a balloon was slipped over the top of an empty pop bottle. Then the bottle was placed in a pan of water, and the water was heated. What do you think will happen next? Why will that happen?

Follow the steps below to see if you are right, then check yourself by reading the solution at the bottom of the page. You'll need a glass bottle (be sure it isn't cracked), a saucepan and a stove (or an electric frying pan), water, and a balloon with a neck large enough to fit over the top of the bottle.

1 *Fill the saucepan with an inch or so of water and put it on a burner of the stove. Or if you're using an electric frying pan, fill it with an inch or so of water and plug it in.*

2 *Slip the balloon's neck over the top of the bottle. Be sure it fits snugly. Set the bottle in the pan of water. Turn the burner on or set the pan to medium heat.*

3 *Observe what happens. Be sure to add water as needed so the pan doesn't go dry.*

SOLUTION:

As the bottle is heated, the air inside becomes warm. Then the air molecules begin to move faster, bumping into each other and bouncing apart. With its molecules more spread out, the air is lighter and rises. As the balloon traps this escaping air, it inflates.

When air cools, the molecules move closer together, making the air heavier. You can prove this. Use a pot holder to lift the bottle out of the pan. Check it after five minutes and again after ten minutes. The balloon will gradually become smaller as the air inside it cools and sinks back down into the bottle.

4.
The Plate Trick

Does air exert pressure in all directions? This experiment is a test to find out. A plastic glass was filled with water. Next, a paper plate was placed upside down over the top of the glass. Then the glass and plate were turned over, with the plate held against the glass like a lid. The boy is about to take his hand away from the plate. What will happen next?

THE PLATE TRICK SOLUTION

You can try this experiment yourself to find out what happens. You'll need a clear plastic glass, water, a paper towel, and a stiff paper plate. When you follow the steps below, you'll want to work over a sink. Don't miss the explanation at the bottom of the page.

1 *Fill the glass nearly full of water. Fold the paper towel and put it on the plate. Place the paper plate and towel upside down over the glass, like a lid.*

2 *Hold the glass in one hand. Press the plate and towel against the glass with the other hand as you turn them over together.*

3 *The glass should be held straight up and down. Slowly take your other hand away from the plate.*

SOLUTION:

Even though air is invisible, it has weight. At the earth's surface, you are at the bottom of a whole column of air extending up through the atmosphere. The average air pressure at the earth's surface is 14.7 pounds per square inch. Air doesn't just push down, though. Air exerts its force in all directions. The plate holds the water in the glass because the force of the air pushing up on a large surface area is much greater than that of the water inside the glass pushing down. The paper towel makes a tight seal between the glass and the plate. This keeps air from slipping inside to help push the water out. If that happened, you'd get wet!

5.
The Big Blow

Does fast-moving air have more or less pressure than slow-moving air? The girl pictured below is holding a long strip of paper just below her lower lip. She blows hard across the top of the strip. What will happen next? Will the paper move up or down?

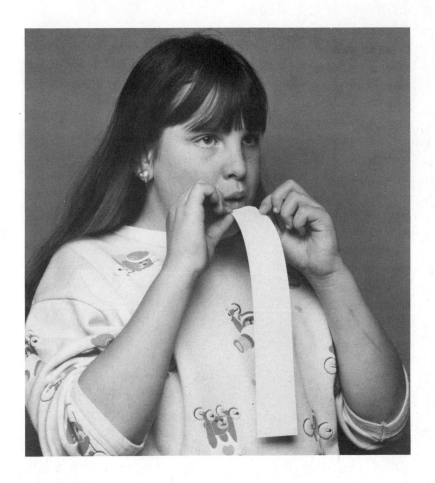

THE BIG BLOW SOLUTION

You can try this experiment to find out if you were right. You'll need scissors, a ruler, and a sheet of notebook paper. Cut a 2-inch-wide strip from the long side of the paper. Keeping your fingers on the very edge of the paper, hold the strip just below your lower lip as shown. Then blow hard down across the top of the strip. Watch what happens to the free end of the strip as you blow. Then read the explanation at the bottom of the page.

SOLUTION:

Although air exerts pressure in all directions, fast-moving air exerts less pressure than slow-moving air. So the fast-moving air from your puff exerts less pressure down on top of the paper than the slow-moving air pushing up from below, and the paper rises.

6.
Undercover Operation

Can you figure out a way to make the balloon lift the book?

Collect a large rubber balloon and a small- to medium-sized book so you can experiment. Then check yourself by reading the solution at the bottom of the page.

SOLUTION:

Air takes up space. So place the balloon under the book with just the neck sticking out and blow into it. As the balloon inflates, the book will be lifted.

7.
Burned Out

Does a fire need oxygen in order to burn? The pictures show what happened in an experiment that was done to find out. But the pictures are out of order. What happened first? Next? Last?

BURNED OUT SOLUTION

To see if you picked the right order for the pictures, you'll need to try the experiment yourself. Collect three birthday candles, three balls of modeling clay, a metal cookie sheet, a glass quart jar, a glass pint jar, and matches. Follow the steps below. Then check the solution.

1 *Put the three balls of clay in a line across the cookie sheet, spaced as far apart as possible. Stick one candle into each.*

2 *Light all three candles. Immediately turn the pint jar upside down over the middle candle. Turn the quart jar upside down over the third candle. Watch closely. You may want to time how long each candle burns.*

SOLUTION:

A fire must have oxygen in order to burn. Usually a fire gets the oxygen it needs from the air around it. As the oxygen in the air is used up, new air containing oxygen rushes in to replace it. However, in an enclosed space, such as inside the jars, the oxygen supply is limited. The candle burns longer inside the larger jar because there is more trapped oxygen.

Did you know that the space shuttle carries a supply of oxygen that is mixed with its fuel during launch? Its three main engines use oxygen so quickly that the air around the shuttle can't supply enough. Also, the shuttle quickly reaches a level in the atmosphere where there is very little oxygen. The thrusters that propel the shuttle while it's in space also use a special type of fuel that contains oxygen.

8.
The Case of the Mystery Message

Have a friend use an artist's paintbrush or a cotton swab and real lemon juice to paint a one-word message on a sheet of paper. No fair peeking. When the message is dry it will be invisible— or nearly so. By using one of the methods shown below, you can cause the lemon-juice writing to change color and become clearly visible. Which method do you think will do the trick?

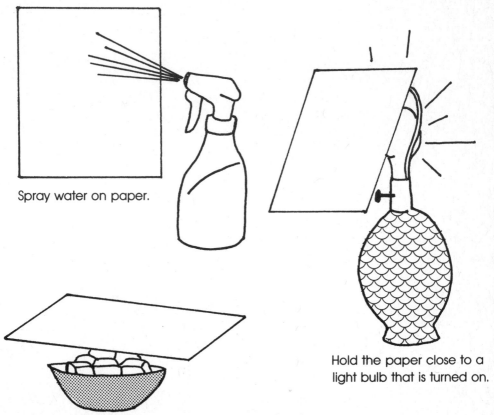

Spray water on paper.

Hold the paper close to a light bulb that is turned on.

Hold the paper close to a bowl of ice cubes.

You'll want to try the method you picked to see if you are correct. You'll need a piece of notebook paper, an artist's paintbrush or a cotton swab, real lemon juice, and a friend. Depending on which method you picked, you'll need either a spray bottle of water, ice cubes, or a lamp with a light bulb that can be turned on. Have your friend secretly write a one-word message, then let the paper dry before you look at it. You may want to have your friend write three separate messages on three separate sheets of paper so you can test what happens with each of the methods. If you try the light bulb, be careful. The bulb will be hot, so don't let the paper or your fingers get too close to it. Be sure to check the explanation at the bottom of the page.

SOLUTION:

Most citrus fruit juices and even onion juice can be used as "invisible" inks. When the paper is heated slowly by the light bulb, chemical compounds in the juice that are normally colorless turn brown.

9.
The Case of the Unattractive Magnet

The directions said to rub the iron nail with a magnet twenty-five times. This was supposed to make the iron nail magnetic, too. But after rubbing the magnet back and forth along the nail twenty-five times, the nail still would not pick up a single paper clip. Why did this investigation fail? What can be done to make the nail magnetic?

THE CASE OF THE UNATTRACTIVE MAGNET SOLUTION

To solve this science mystery, you need to understand what happens to make metals, such as iron, magnetic. Collect a bar magnet (be sure it's strong enough to attract at least fifteen paper clips), an iron nail, and a box of steel paper clips. Try out what you think should be done to magnetize the nail. Then check yourself by reading the solution at the bottom of the page.

SOLUTION:

Like all matter, iron is made up of tiny building blocks called atoms. When the atoms in iron can be made to arrange themselves in an orderly manner, the metal becomes magnetic. One way that the atoms can be made to line up in the iron nail is to rub it *in one direction only* with a magnet. This investigation failed because the iron nail was rubbed back and forth.

10.
The Clip Caper

Look at the picture closely. The copper wire is coiled around an iron nail. When the ends of the wire are attached to a battery, the nail becomes a magnet. This special kind of magnet is called an electromagnet. There are fifteen metal paper clips in the clump that the electromagnet is able to pick up. It won't pick up any more than fifteen clips—the extras just fall off. Without using any additional materials, how can you change the electromagnet to make it strong enough to pick up more than fifteen clips?

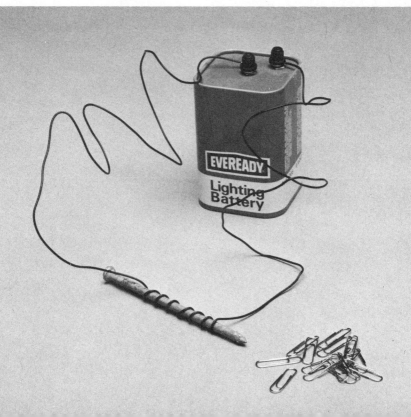

THE CLIP CAPER SOLUTION

You can build an electromagnet so you can try out your ideas for how to make it stronger. Collect a 6-volt battery with screw-down terminals, 24 inches of insulated copper wire, scissors, electrician's tape, an iron nail, and a box of steel paper clips. Follow the steps below to assemble an electromagnet like the one in the picture. Experiment. Then check the solution at the bottom of the page.

1 *Use the scissors to strip about an inch of insulation off each end of the wire.*

2 *Wrap the wire around the nail five times. Attach one bare wire end to one of the battery's terminals. Attach the other end of the wire to the other terminal. This starts an electric current flowing through the wire and makes the nail an electromagnet. Pull one end of the wire away from the battery any time you want to switch off the magnet.*

3 *Test your electromagnet to see how many paper clips it will pick up. It may pick up more than fifteen clips or it may pick up less. Then try all the ways you can think of to make the electromagnet stronger.*

SOLUTION:

An electric current, like a magnet, has an invisible magnetic force field around it. To make the electromagnet stronger, you can wrap more coils around the nail. These additional coils will each have electricity flowing through them. So there will be more lines of force in the magnetic field.

11.
In Search of the Invisible Force

The ends of magnets are called poles. One is called the north pole, because if the magnet were suspended and allowed to swing freely, it would point toward the earth's magnetic north pole. The opposite end of the magnet, then, is called the south pole. When this sheet of paper was sprinkled with iron filings, it was suddenly possible to see the outlines of the two magnets hidden underneath. The iron filings were attracted to the magnets' invisible lines of force, outlining them. Look closely. Do the hidden magnets have two unlike poles (N–S) or two like poles (N–N or S–S) facing each other?

CLUE: Think about how like and unlike poles of magnets react to each other.

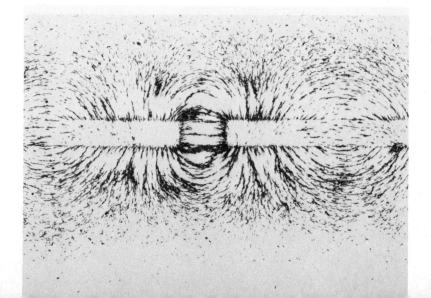

Did you decide that the mystery magnets have like poles facing each other? You'll need to repeat this experiment to see how the lines of force really appear when the like poles of two magnets are facing. Collect a newspaper, a sheet of notebook paper, two bar magnets, and iron filings (available from a hobby supply shop or can be borrowed from a science teacher). Follow the steps below and compare the results to what you saw in the mystery picture. Then check the solution at the bottom of the page.

1 *Spread out the newspaper. Place the two magnets about two inches apart. Position them with either their N–N or S–S poles facing each other.*

2 *Cover the magnets with the sheet of notebook paper, then slowly sprinkle on the iron filings.*

SOLUTION:

Like poles of a magnet repel each other. Unlike poles attract. When you tried the experiment with like poles facing, the lines of force from each magnet stopped midway, as if there were an invisible wall between the two magnets. The lines of force in the picture, however, curve from one magnet to the other, showing attraction. So the hidden magnets have unlike poles facing. If you haven't already tried it, sprinkle filings on a paper covering magnets with unlike (N–S) poles facing. Then you'll be able to see the lines of force curving between the two magnets.

12.
Going Around in Circuits

In this experiment, the goal is to build a complete electric circuit. The word *circuit* means circle. The flow of tiny charged particles called electrons is electricity. When electricity can be made to flow from a power source through a filament (the thin wire inside a light bulb) and back to the power source, a complete circuit is created. The friction caused by electrons squeezing through the filament makes this wire white-hot, and it glows.

Which of these two setups is a complete circuit that will make the light bulb glow?

A   B

You'll need to build the circuit you picked to see if it really does light up the bulb. Collect aluminum foil, inch-wide transparent tape, scissors, a D-cell battery, and a flashlight bulb. To make the foil wire, put about a 12- to 14-inch strip of tape on the dull side of a sheet of aluminum foil. Cut out the foil along either side of the tape. Next, fold the wire in half so the two tape sides are together. Then, follow the steps to build either Circuit A or Circuit B. If the circuit you picked doesn't light the bulb, try the other one. Maybe neither of these two circuits is complete. Or they could both be complete. Check the solution below.

Circuit A
1 *Sit the indented end of the battery on the foil wire.*

2 *Wrap the free end of the wire around the bulb's screw base.*

3 *Touch the metal tip of the bulb to the knob top of the battery.*

Circuit B
1-2 *Just like Circuit A.*

3 *Touch the glass top of the bulb to the knob top of the battery.*

SOLUTION: Only Circuit A is a complete circuit and will make the bulb light. To be a complete circuit, the electrons must flow in through the metal tip of the bulb and out through its grooved metal base. The metal is a good conductor of electricity, but the glass does not conduct electricity. So when the glass is touching the battery, the electrons can't flow into the bulb.

13.
That's Bright

Which of the two diagrams below illustrates the circuit that will make the bulb glow the brightest? Use the key showing the common electrical symbols to help you understand the diagrams.

CLUE: Think about how the electricity will be moving through each circuit.

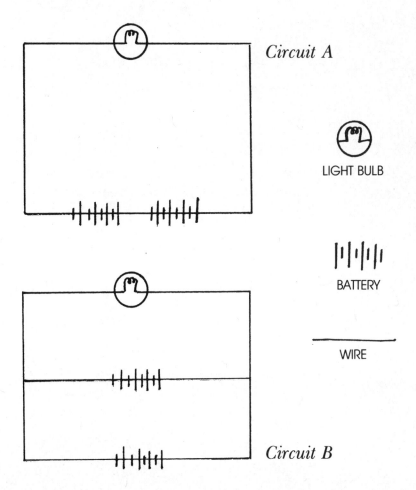

Circuit A

LIGHT BULB

BATTERY

WIRE

Circuit B

THAT'S BRIGHT SOLUTION

You'll need to build both circuits to compare the bulb's brightness and see if you were right. Collect four D-cell batteries, two flashlight bulbs, two 20-inch-long foil wires (made following the directions in Going Around in Circuits). Connect each circuit as shown in the picture. Then check the solution at the bottom of the page.

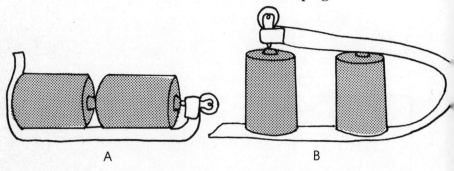

A   B

SOLUTION:

The batteries in Circuit A are said to be connected in parallel because the combined batteries act like a single unit. The flow of electrons to the bulb isn't any greater than it would be with one battery. So the bulb won't burn any brighter. However, because each battery is sharing the job of supplying energy, the batteries will last longer. The batteries in Circuit B are said to be connected in series. This arrangement increases the electron flow pushing through the thin wire filament inside the bulb. The bulb glows more brightly than usual, but both the bulb and the batteries will burn out more quickly.

14.
It's a Holdup!

The sheet of paper was placed like a bridge across the two cups. But when a third cup was put on top, and pennies added one at a time, the paper quickly collapsed. How could you change this sheet of paper to make it strong enough to support the cup and at least ten pennies?

IT'S A HOLDUP! SOLUTION

You'll want to experiment to test your ideas. So collect three Styrofoam cups, twenty pennies, a ruler, and plenty of sheets of notebook paper. Place two of the cups 6 inches apart to support the paper. Each time you do a test, place the paper over the two cups. Then carefully put the other cup on top of this paper bridge and add the pennies, one at a time. Keep a record of how many pennies each paper bridge will support. Which design is the strongest? Check the solution at the bottom of the page.

SOLUTION:

Fold the paper accordion-style, as shown. Adding pleats makes the paper less flexible and more resistant to bending. The bigger the folds the more rigid the paper becomes. Try it. Fold one paper bridge with a few big, deep pleats. Fold another with shallow pleats. Then test to find out which will support more weight.

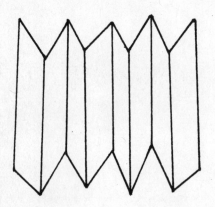
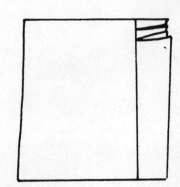

15.
The Handkerchief Trick

Without using any other materials than the ones shown, can you think of a way to get the rock salt through the handkerchief without tearing the cloth?

THE HANDKERCHIEF TRICK SOLUTION

Do you have an idea how to solve this mystery? Experiment to see if you're right. Collect a handkerchief (be sure it's one you are allowed to use), ¼ cup of rock salt (available at grocery stores), a bowl, a quart jar, a rubber band, a long-handled spoon, and a pitcher of water. Don't miss the solution at the bottom of the page.

SOLUTION:

Many solid materials will dissolve in water—including rock-hard chunks of salt. Pour the salt into the bowl, add enough water to cover the salt, and stir with the long-handled spoon. The salt will slowly dissolve, breaking down until its molecules are suspended in the water. Next, put the handkerchief over the top of the jar and anchor it in place with the rubber band. If you look at the cloth with a magnifying glass, you'll see spaces between the crisscrossed woven threads. Pour the salty water slowly onto the handkerchief. The water carries the salt molecules through these spaces. You can see the salty water dripping into the jar. The handkerchief remains undamaged.

16.
The Case of the Leaky Can

The can below has three holes—A, B, and C. When the can is filled with water, will it spurt the same distance from all three holes? Or, if not, from which hole will the water spray the farthest?

CLUE: Think what affects water pressure.

Try this experiment yourself to find out if you were right about the spurts. Then check the explanation at the bottom of the page. You'll need a 3-pound metal can (the kind that coffee or vegetable shortening comes in), a piece of 2 × 4 wood, long enough to anchor on a table or workbench, a clamp, a large steel nail, a hammer, sandpaper, and a pitcher of water. (You may want an adult's help when punching the holes in the can.)

1 *Put the wood on a table or workbench so one end sticks out over the edge. Anchor the other end with the clamp (be sure you have permission to do so). Next, place the can over the free end, holding the side of the can against the wood.*

2 *Hammer a nail straight through the can just into the wood. Then pull out the nail. Make the hole as round as possible. Repeat to make two more holes in a vertical line with the first. Space the holes about 2 inches apart. Rub sandpaper over the edges of the holes to make the metal smooth.*

3 *Place the can on the side of a sink with the holes aimed at the sink. Quickly pour in enough water to fill the can and observe.*

SOLUTION:

Water has weight. The weight pushing downward makes the pressure at the bottom of the column of water greatest. So the water spurts the farthest from C, the bottom hole. Do you think there would be any difference in the strength of the streams of water spurting out if the holes were horizontal—all at the same level—instead of vertical? Try it and find out.

17.
Juice Sleuth

Acids and bases are two groups of chemicals. Weak acids are found in fruit juices and tea. They give foods a sharp taste. Weak bases are used in many cleaning products because their chemical structure makes them slippery and soapy. One base used in foods is baking soda.

Because of the way other chemicals react when they're mixed with an acid or a base, sometimes it's important to identify these chemicals. Grape juice has the special ability to change color when it's mixed with an acid or a base, so it is called an indicator. With an acid, grape juice becomes light red. With a base, it turns dark green. The juice stays purple if it's mixed with a chemical that is neither an acid nor a base. Such a chemical is said to be neutral.

Grape juice is about to be added to each of these cups. It will reveal whether a cup contains an acid, a base, or a neutral chemical. What color will this indicator turn in each case?

GRAPE JUICE

AMMONIA

WATER   VINEGAR   JUICE

JUICE SLEUTH SOLUTION

You can do this experiment to see the color changes for yourself. You'll need real grape juice, white vinegar, ammonia, lemon juice, water, five clear glasses, a tablespoon, and a measuring cup. Follow the steps below to discover what happens. Then check the solution below.

1 *Put the grape juice indicator solution in one glass. To prepare, mix one part grape juice with nine parts water. For example, add 1 tablespoon of grape juice for every 9 tablespoons of water.*

2 *Set four glasses in a row. Pour ¼ cup of water into the first glass, ¼ cup of vinegar into the second, ¼ cup of lemon juice into the third, ¼ cup of ammonia into the last glass.*

3 *Pour 3 tablespoons of indicator into each glass. Jiggle the glass slightly to mix the liquids, then observe the color.*

SOLUTION:

Vinegar and lemon juice are acids. So the indicator turns light red in these. Ammonia is a base, making the indicator turn dark green. Water is neutral, so the indicator stays light purple. Now try testing other mystery solutions to see if they are acid, base, or neutral.

When just the right amount of an acid is mixed with a base, the solution becomes neutral. Can you develop an experiment that would let you find out how many drops of vinegar it would take to neutralize ¼ cup of ammonia? You would need to test your solution with the indicator.

18.
Good Cents

Here are the materials that are to be used for this experiment. What will happen when they are put together?

SALT

VINEGAR

DIRTY PENNIES

PAPER PLATE

GOOD CENTS SOLUTION

You'll want to put these materials together to discover what does happen. Then read the explanation at the bottom of the page. You'll need a plate (even a heavy paper plate will do), five discolored pennies, ¼ cup of vinegar, and 2 tablespoons of salt.

1 *Place the pennies on the plate. Put them close together but don't let them overlap.*

2 *Sprinkle the salt evenly over the pennies and then pour on the vinegar. Make sure some vinegar wets each penny.*

SOLUTION:

When copper is in contact with the air for a while, it changes to copper compounds that appear dark. That's what has happened to discolor the pennies. Salt contains chloride atoms. When these chloride atoms are present in a weak acid solution, such as vinegar, they cause the copper compounds on the pennies to dissolve easily. As these compounds move into the vinegar solution, a fresh, shiny layer of copper becomes visible.

19.
The Case of the Hot Thermometer

Does insulation trap heat? This experiment would let you find out, but something is missing. Look at the picture closely. Can you spot what needs to be included in this experiment?

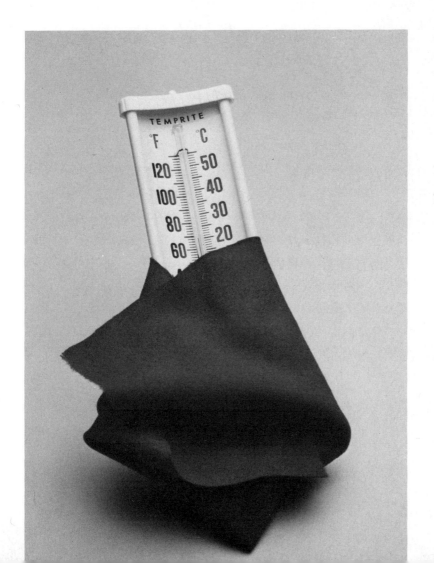

THE CASE OF THE HOT THERMOMETER SOLUTION

Did you guess what's missing? If not, follow the steps below to do the experiment as it's shown in the picture. This should help you spot what has been left out. Check yourself by reading the solution at the bottom of the page. You'll need a 12-inch square of thin wool cloth, an indoor/outdoor thermometer, a pint jar, hot water, a clock, and a refrigerator.

1 *Fill the jar halfway with hot water. Put the bulb end of the thermometer into the water and let it sit for five minutes. Check the temperature.*

2 *Wrap the thermometer in the wool and put it in the refrigerator for five minutes. Check the new temperature.*

3 *Decide if insulation does prevent heat loss.*

SOLUTION:

The control—the part of an experiment used for comparison—is missing. To add a control, you need to use two thermometers—one that is wrapped and one that is unwrapped. Then you can compare whether the insulated thermometer loses heat less rapidly than the one that is unprotected.

20.
The Little Chill

You know that a breeze cools you off. But if your skin was wet when the wind was blowing, would you feel even cooler? How could you use the materials shown below to find out?

CLUE: Think about what you need to do to design an experiment. For more information, read page 1.

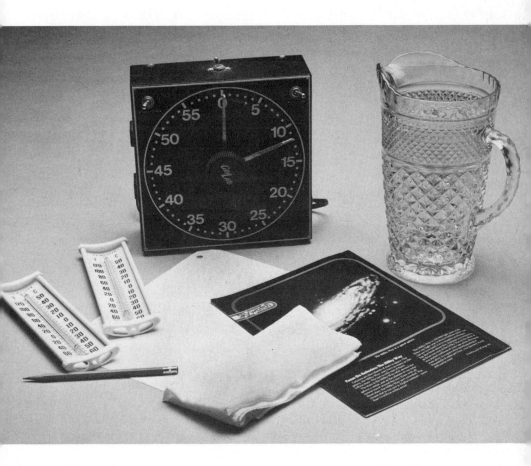

To try out the experiment you design, you'll need the materials shown in the picture: water, a 6-inch square of cotton cloth, two indoor/outdoor thermometers, a pencil, a clock with a second hand, a magazine, and a sheet of notebook paper. Be sure to check the solution below.

SOLUTION:

Here is one possible experiment design.

Define problem: "What will increase the wind's cooling effect?"

State hypothesis: Being wet will increase the wind's cooling effect.

Choose materials: Use items in the picture.

Experiment and collect data: Wet the cloth and squeeze it out. Check and record the temperature on both thermometers. Place the thermometers side by side in a warm, shady location. Cover the bulb end of one thermometer with the wet cloth. Use the magazine to fan both with slow, steady strokes. Check and record the temperature after one minute and again after two minutes. (When you do your experiment, you'll need to list the temperature readings you discover.) Repeat three times.

Draw a conclusion: Being wet does increase the wind's cooling effect. The temperature of both thermometers went down when they were fanned, but the one with the wet bulb always showed the greatest heat loss. Moving air speeds up evaporation, the process of a liquid changing to a gas. And evaporation uses up heat energy.

21.
The Paper Towel Caper

This experiment is supposed to be testing which paper towel soaks up water fastest, but it's not a good test. Can you spot what's wrong?

CLUE: Think about good scientific method. You can read more about it on page 1.

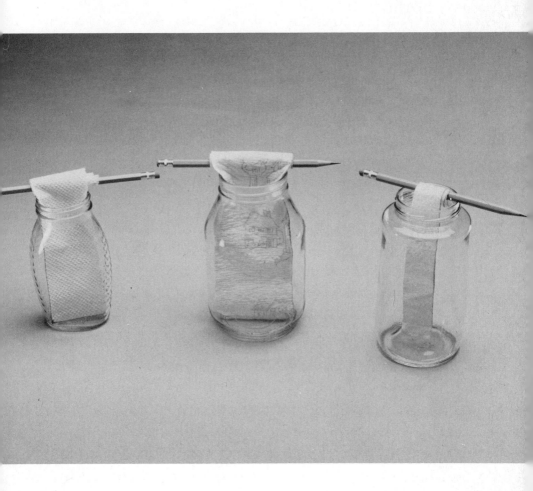

THE PAPER TOWEL CAPER SOLUTION

Doing the experiment just the way it's shown in the picture will help you see what's wrong. So collect three different brands of paper towels, three different-sized containers that are no more than 10 inches tall, a measuring cup, a pitcher of water, scissors, three pencils, tape, a ruler, a ballpoint pen, and a clock with a second hand. Follow the steps below. Then check the solution at the bottom of the page.

1 *Put ½ cup of water in each different container.*

2 *Cut a strip 1 × 10 inches from one towel, a strip 2 × 10 inches from another towel, and a strip 3 × 10 inches from the third towel. Tape one end of each strip to a pencil. As close to the same time as possible, place one towel strip into each container so the free end just touches the water. You may need to roll the strip around the pencil to shorten it.*

3 *After one minute, use the pen to mark how high the water has traveled up each strip. Then compare to decide which strip soaked up water the fastest. Think about what you've just done. Decide why you really can't tell which towel soaked up water fastest based on this experiment.*

SOLUTION:

For you to be able to make a comparison, all the towel strips need to be exactly the same size and all the containers of water need to be exactly alike. Then the only difference will be the towels' ability to absorb water. Now, control all the variables and repeat this test to find out which towel really does the best job.

22.
The Balloon Trick

Both of these balloons were rubbed with wool. Look what happened. How do you think it would change the results if you sprayed both balloons with water?

The only way to know for sure is to try the experiment yourself. You'll need two rubber balloons, two 14-inch pieces of string, a piece of wool cloth, a yardstick, a table, books, and a spray bottle filled with water. Follow the steps below, then check the solution below.

1 *Blow up the balloons, knot to seal, and tie a piece of string around each neck. Anchor a yardstick to a table with a stack of books. Tie the free end of each string around the yardstick, making sure the balloons hang side by side, almost touching.*

2 *Rub each balloon with the wool, using quick, short strokes. When the balloons repel each other, lightly spray them with water. Observe.*

SOLUTION:

All matter is made up of atoms, and all atoms are made up of even tinier particles called neutrons, protons, and electrons. Neutrons and protons remain tightly bound, but the electrons of some atoms can be easily knocked loose. Rubbing makes some electrons from the wool join some of the atoms on the balloon.

When atoms don't have an equal number of electrons and protons, they become electrically charged. Atoms like those on the balloon that have extra electrons—more electrons than the number of protons—are said to be negatively charged. And just the way the poles of magnets respond, objects with the same electrical charge repel each other. The water droplets pick up the extra electrons from the balloons. So when they're sprayed, the balloons drop back together.

23.
The Mysterious Floating Egg

Look closely. The egg is floating, suspended in the middle of a quart jar filled with water. Normally the egg would sink to the bottom. Which of the materials shown beside the jar do you think was added to the water to make the egg float?

SUGAR

OIL

SALT

THE MYSTERIOUS FLOATING EGG SOLUTION

You can experiment to find out if you are right. Collect a quart jar, water, an uncooked egg (be sure it doesn't have any cracks), a serving spoon, a cup of sugar, a cup of oil, and a cup of salt. Each time you make a test, fill the jar two-thirds full of water. Next, add 1 cup of a test material and stir well. Then ease the egg into the water. If the egg doesn't float, remove it and empty the jar. Rinse the jar well and repeat the test with the next material. When you've discovered the solution, check the explanation at the bottom of the page.

SOLUTION:

Both sugar and salt make the egg float because they increase the density—the thickness—of the water. If you've ever been swimming in the ocean, you know how much easier it is to float in salty water than in fresh water. If the amount of salt or sugar you added didn't make your egg float right in the center of the jar, you can adjust the water's density. Carefully remove the egg and add more salt or sugar if the water needs to be denser. Then ease the egg back into the water.

24.
Dirty Business

This soil is made up of particles that are three different sizes. How could you use the equipment shown in the picture to separate the soil particles into separate layers?

DIRTY BUSINESS SOLUTION

You'll want to experiment, so collect a quart jar, a pitcher of water, a long-handled spoon, and 2 cups of soil. Be sure the soil obviously contains particles that are different sizes, or mix together several different soil samples. Then check the solution at the bottom of the page.

SOLUTION:

When particles are mixed in water, they soon begin to settle to the bottom. The biggest, heaviest particles sink first. So all you need to do to separate the soil particles is to dump the soil into the jar, add some water, and stir with the long-handled spoon. Try it. You'll need to let the dirty water sit for at least an hour. Then look closely. You will be able to see distinct layers of soil particles.

25.
Beans in the Dark

One of these two pots of bean plants sprouted and grew in a dark closet. Which pot of beans do you think grew in the dark? Why did you make that choice?

What do you think will happen to the beans that were grown in the dark if they are moved into the sunlight?

A   B

BEANS IN THE DARK SOLUTION

You can grow a cup full of beans in the dark to see what they look like. Collect dried beans (soup beans that you can buy at a grocery store), a Styrofoam cup, a pitcher of water, a pencil, a metal pie pan, and enough potting soil to fill the cup. Then follow the steps below. After you've discovered what happens, check the explanation below. Finally, move the bean plants into the sunlight to find out how they change.

1 *Put six beans in the cup and pour in enough water to cover the seeds. Let them sit overnight. This softens the seed coat and makes the seeds sprout faster.*

2 *Next dump out the water. Set the seeds aside. Poke several small drainage holes in the bottom of the cup with the pencil. Then set the cup on the pie pan, fill it with potting soil, and bury the seeds just below the surface of the soil. Sprinkle on enough water to moisten the soil and place the pie pan with the cup on it in a warm, dark closet. Check every couple of days, adding water as needed to keep the soil moist.*

SOLUTION:

Plant cells have special light receptors. When they don't receive light, they signal the plant cells to grow long and thin. The plants are actually seeking the light they need to produce food. Once these receptors begin to receive light, they signal the cells to grow in a sturdier way. Plants grown in the dark also don't produce a normal amount of chlorophyll, the chemical that makes plants green. So the beans grown in the dark are very pale—almost white. But after they are moved into the light, the plants become green.

26.
Bean Magic

This plastic pill bottle was packed with dry bean seeds. Next, enough water was poured in to fill up all the spaces, and the cap was put on tightly. What do you think will happen to the bottle full of beans when it is left overnight?

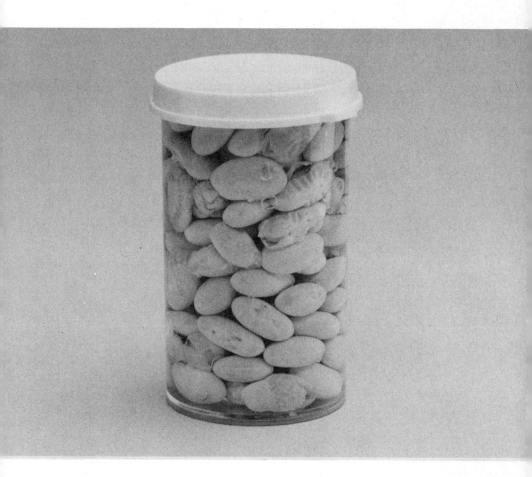

BEAN MAGIC SOLUTION

Do you know? Try the experiment to see what happens. You'll need bean seeds (dried beans that are available at grocery store), a plastic pill bottle with a lid that snaps on, and water. Pack the pill bottle full of dried beans and pour in enough water to fill in all the spaces. Close the lid securely and let the bottle sit overnight. After you've discovered what happens, read the explanation at the bottom of the page.

SOLUTION:

If you look closely at a dried bean, you'll see a tiny hole on the indented side. This hole lets water into the seed. When wet, the seed coat softens, and the seed leaves swell. The seed leaves will supply the young plant with food as it first starts to grow. The pressure exerted as these plant tissues swell is a strong force. It's enough either to pop off the cap or to crack the sides of the plastic pill bottle. Once it was even enough to sink a ship.

During World War II, a ship carrying sacks of food was torpedoed. The damage wasn't severe. So the ship continued on its way. However, dried beans that had been soaked began to swell. Eventually, the pressure became so great that the ship's hull split open, and the ship sank.

SEED LEAVES

YOUNG PLANT

SEED COAT

LITTLE HOLE FOR WATER TO ENTER

27.
Spoiled Rotten

This experiment was supposed to test if fertilizer makes plants grow bigger, but it failed. Look at the furry mold growing on the soil. The beans didn't sprout. What happened to ruin this experiment?

CLUE: Think about what conditions seeds need to sprout.

SPOILED ROTTEN SOLUTION

Did you guess that the bean seeds received too much water? To find out if you're right, repeat the experiment but make the amount of water the variable to be tested. You'll need two Styrofoam cups, potting soil, a sturdy paper plate, a pencil, twelve bean seeds (dried beans available at grocery store), a bowl, water, a pipe cleaner, and a tablespoon. Next, follow the steps below to set up the experiment. Then check the explanation at the bottom of the page.

1 *Put the bean seeds in the bowl. Pour on enough water to cover the seeds and let them sit overnight. This softens the seed coat and makes the seeds sprout faster.*

2 *Use the pencil to poke drainage holes in the bottom of both cups. Set the cups side by side on the paper plate and fill them with potting soil. Plant six seeds just below the surface in each cup. Mark the test cup with a pipe-cleaner flag. Pour 1 tablespoon of water on the unmarked cup. This cup is the control, the part of the experiment that shows what happens under normal conditions. Pour 4 tablespoons of water on the other cup.*

3 *Add 1 tablespoon of water to the unmarked cup every third day. Add 4 tablespoons of water to the other cup daily.*

SOLUTION:

Seeds need water for the young plants to start to grow, but they also need oxygen. Too much water keeps developing plants from getting enough oxygen, and they won't sprout. The extra moisture also encourages mold growth, and the seeds rot.

28.
The Case of the Changing Carnation

Examine these materials carefully. How could you use them to change the white carnation to one that is half red and half blue?

THE CASE OF THE CHANGING CARNATION SOLUTION

When you think you know what to do, try your idea. Collect two pill bottles, a sharp kitchen knife, water, a bottle of red food coloring, a bottle of blue food coloring, and a white carnation. (If you can't get a white carnation, you can use a stalk of celery. However, celery is stiffer and harder to work with. And because celery is green, the color change will be less obvious.) You may want an adult to help you do any cutting you decide is needed. Check yourself by reading the solution at the bottom of the page.

SOLUTION:

Plants have tubes, called xylem tubes, that carry water up through the plant. Moisture evaporating—moving into the air—from the surfaces of leaves and flower petals creates a pull on the water within the plant's xylem tubes. This force is strong enough to draw water up many feet—even to the top of a tall tree—despite the downward pull of gravity. Because water molecules cling together, a whole column of water rises in the tube. To create a carnation that is half red and half blue, follow the steps below.

1 *Cut off the tip of the stem to open the xylem tubes. Then carefully split the stem in half up about four inches.*

2 *Fill each pill bottle with water. Put 3 drops of red food coloring in one and 3 drops of blue food coloring in the other. Place one-half of the stem in each bottle. Let the flower sit overnight.*

29.
The Green Thumb Caper

This experiment was supposed to test whether fertilizer makes plants grow taller. However, the experiment doesn't use good scientific method, so the results won't provide any useful information. Can you spot what's wrong? What could be changed to make this test successful?

CLUE: You can read more about good scientific method on p. 1.

FERTILIZER WATER

PLAIN WATER

THE GREEN THUMB CAPER SOLUTION

Are you still not sure what's wrong? Then look at the picture of the experiment closely to answer each of these questions.

1 *What are the variables? Are all the variables controlled?*

2 *How many times are the test and the control being performed?*

Think you've got the solution now? Then check the explanation at the bottom of the page.

SOLUTION:

To be a good experiment, all the variables except the one being tested need to be the same for the test and the control plants. So the plants should be the same kind and size. They should be in identical pots containing the same amount and type of soil. And they should be placed side by side in a warm, sunny spot so they'll be exposed to the same temperature and amount of sunlight. Finally, both plants should receive the same amount of water. The only difference should be that the water for the test plant also contains fertilizer.

Then the test and the control need to be repeated. With only one test plant and one control plant, the results aren't useful even if all the variables are carefully controlled. Either the test or the control plant might just grow unusually fast or slow. There should be at least three test plants and three control plants. Then, if the results were the same or nearly the same for all the test plants and all the control plants, you'd know the information was reliable.

60

Congratulations!

Having solved all these mysteries, you are now a science supersleuth. But don't stop experimenting. There's a world full of science mysteries that need solving, and you've discovered a whole new way of digging into puzzling situations.

The next time you see a piece of moldy fruit, try to track down what went wrong. Or see if you can discover a way to keep other fruit from spoiling.

Collect interesting items and try to think of all the ways those items could interact with each other. Then test some of your ideas.

Watch how things work, think of changes that might make them work even better—and experiment.

There's still a lot of action waiting for you. Just be a good observer, and you'll soon be working on your next science mystery.

Designing a Science Experiment

Part of being a good science detective is finding new cases to solve. Since you're curious and observant, you won't have any trouble digging up things to explore. When you do, following these five basic steps will help you design a successful experiment.

1 *Define the problem.* It should be stated as a question. Then you know what answer you're trying to find.

2 *State a hypothesis.* This will be your guess about what variable—condition that can change—could be causing the problem. For example, the problem could be "What affects erosion?" Then a possible hypothesis would be "The greater the slope the faster soil erodes." As you can see, a problem is often very general. The hypothesis, though, is very specific. Then your experiment is a test to find out if your hypothesis is correct.

3 *Choose the materials to use in your experiment.* Think about what you will need to do your test, and make sure these items are inexpensive, readily available, and safe for you to use.

4 *Perform the test and collect the data.* You need to use good scientific method as you work. Be a good observer, measure carefully, and record all information neatly.

5 *Draw a conclusion based on the data you collected.* This conclusion should very briefly state if your hypothesis was correct or not. If your hypothesis was not correct, it should offer a suggestion for a new guess to test.

Index